BLACK OPS
AND OTHER SPECIAL
MISSIONS OF THE
U.S. NAVY
SEALS

Simone Payment

rosen publishing's
rosen central

New York

Published in 2013 by The Rosen Publishing Group, Inc.
29 East 21st Street, New York, NY 10010

Library of Congress Cataloging-in-Publication Data

Payment, Simone.
Black ops and other special missions of the U.S. Navy SEALs/Simone Payment.—1st ed.
     p. cm.—(Inside Special Forces)
Includes bibliographical references and index.
ISBN 978-1-4488-8380-6 (library binding)—
ISBN 978-1-4488-8385-1 (pbk.)—
ISBN 978-1-4488-8386-8 (6-pack)
1. United States. Navy. SEALs—History—21st century—Juvenile literature. I. Title.
VG87.P388 2013
359.9'84—dc23

2012014776

Manufactured in the United States of America

CPSIA Compliance Information: Batch #W13YA: For further information, contact Rosen Publishing, New York, New York, at 1-800-237-9932.

CONTENTS

INTRODUCTION

SNEAKING INTO A WALLED compound in the middle of a pitch-dark night to capture terrorists; crawling through the dusty desert to sneak up on an enemy camp and rescue hostages; parachuting from 30,000 feet (9,144 meters); tracking an enemy through an insect-filled swamp; swimming for miles underwater to reach a shore undetected; hiding on a mountain ledge for hours to catch sight of an enemy on the move—it's all in a day's work for a Navy SEAL.

SEALs are a highly trained, unique group of special operations forces in the U.S. Navy. "SEAL" stands for sea, air, and land. Other special operations forces are trained to serve in specialized conditions. For example, Army Rangers fight in land-based missions. SEALs can fight in any kind of situation. They are extremely focused and can think clearly in high-pressure circumstances. They are so well-trained that they are ready for anything. They plan their missions to the last detail. However, they are always prepared to adjust their plan at a moment's notice, depending on changing conditions during a mission.

The SEALs are a top-secret organization. SEALs do not talk about their work, even with their families. SEALs cannot tell neighbors, or even friends, what they do for a living. When SEALs are deployed on a mission, their families do not know where they are or when they will return. Most of the time, the general public never hears about SEAL missions. It is only when the SEALs have a great success, such as capturing and killing Osama bin Laden, that the SEALs make the news.

The general public also sometimes hears about SEAL missions that have gone wrong in some way, such as when a helicopter was shot down in Afghanistan in August 2011, killing twenty-two SEALs. The rest of the time, the SEALs quietly go about their business, making the world a safer place for everyone.

Many SEAL missions take place under cover of darkness. On night missions, SEALs are outfitted with high-tech equipment, including night-vision goggles.

SEALs are an extremely well-prepared fighting force. A SEAL has at least three years of training before he goes on his first mission. SEAL training is very demanding. The trainees push themselves to the limit, over and over again. Once a trainee becomes a SEAL, training does not stop. Before every mission, SEALs practice what might happen so that they will be prepared for anything that might occur. Between missions, they learn new skills and practice old skills.

SEALs must be on top of their game at all times. If they are not, it can be disastrous for the individual and for the other team members. SEALs depend on each other—their lives are in each other's hands. They come to feel like they are brothers, and they are willing to risk their lives to save their fellow SEALs.

For all their dedication and hard work, SEALs earn few rewards. Their jobs are difficult and dangerous. The hours and weeks they put in are long. The sacrifices they make are big. But for SEALs, the sacrifices and danger and difficulty are their own reward. They are risk takers who like adventure and danger. Most of all, they love pushing themselves to their limits and serving the United States.

BECOMING A SEAL

SEALS ARE A VERY SPECIAL group within the U.S. Navy. They are men from many different backgrounds who are all willing to serve the United States. As Eric Greitens puts it in his book *The Heart and the Fist: The Education of a Humanitarian, the Making of a Navy SEAL*, they are willing to "sacrifice their own pleasures and comforts and even their lives, in service of others."

WHO ARE SEALS?

SEALs are part of the U.S. Naval Special Warfare Command (NSWC). This is part of the larger U.S. Special Operations Command (USSOCOM). USSOCOM oversees special operations forces from other branches of the military, such as the air force and army.

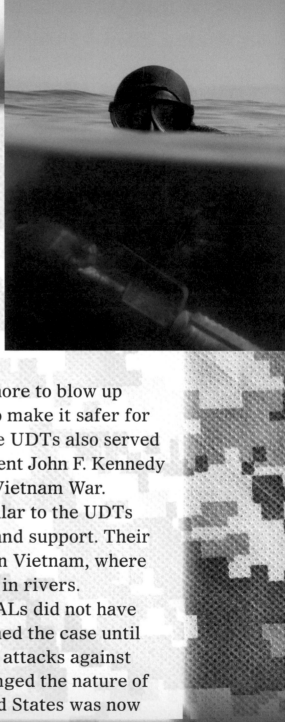

This SEAL is using an oxygen rebreather, which recycles the carbon monoxide he exhales. This system has the advantage of not producing bubbles, which could give away the SEAL's location.

If several special operations teams—such as the Navy SEALs and Army Rangers—are going to work together on a mission, USSOCOM coordinates and helps plan the mission.

SEALs have their history in underwater demolition teams (UDTs) from World War II. These combat teams would go ashore to blow up enemy targets or enemy bombs to make it safer for other troops to enter the area. The UDTs also served in the Korean War. In 1962, President John F. Kennedy formed the SEALs to fight in the Vietnam War. These new SEAL teams were similar to the UDTs but received even more training and support. Their water training served them well in Vietnam, where many battles were fought near or in rivers.

After the Vietnam War, the SEALs did not have as many missions and that remained the case until September 11, 2011. The terrorist attacks against the United States on that day changed the nature of how wars were fought. The United States was now involved in a war on terrorism. In the wars of the past, the United States generally faced large armies fighting battles on land. To fight against terrorists, the military needed small, well-trained units that could get to an area quickly. They would also need to adapt to changing missions and operate secretively and be able to fight on land or sea. SEALs are perfectly suited to meet these needs.

MISSION TYPES

Although SEAL forces are trained to perform in any circumstances, they have four basic types of missions. In direct action missions, the goal is to

SEALs train in various environments, many of which are located far away from towns and cities to avoid giving away their tactics to enemies.

eliminate threats from enemy forces using raids, ambushes, and assaults.

Special reconnaissance missions are for SEALs to observe a location or person (or group) from afar and report back to team leaders. These missions allow SEALs to gather information that can be passed along to other units or larger fighting forces. The third type of mission is counterterrorism. In these missions, SEALs take action against enemy forces to prevent acts of terrorism. The last mission type is foreign internal defense. These missions allow SEALs to train foreign allies so that they can work together

SLOW AND STEADY

Most people's heart rate changes depending on the situation. The heart beats faster in high-stress situations and slower under normal or relaxed conditions. However, some people have a steady heartbeat no matter what the circumstances. These people have what is called a metronomic heartbeat. Researchers have found that these people have a higher level of a certain neurotransmitter in their brains. This substance counteracts the effects of stress hormones and allows the heartbeat to remain steady. People with a metronomic heartbeat can handle high-stress situations calmly. The navy looks for people with metronomic heartbeats when choosing SEAL candidates.

to stop terrorism or other acts of aggression. An unofficial fifth mission is rescuing hostages. This could be considered a subtype of direct action missions.

BUD/S (BASIC UNDERWATER DEMOLITION/SEALS)

The process of becoming a SEAL is an intense one. Only the most physically fit and mentally tough men will make it through SEAL training. To be accepted for SEAL training, candidates must pass several tests. One is the Physical Screening Test (PST), which checks a candidate's physical fitness. To start training, candidates must pass the PST. They must also be twenty-eight or younger, in excellent physi cal condition, and have good eyesight. At the present time, women are not accepted into SEAL training.

SEAL candidates begin the training process at the Naval Special Warfare Center in Coronado, California. There they go through Indoc, which stands for Indoctrination Course. Indoc consists of four to six weeks of running, swimming, and other physical training. This training prepares candidates for what is to come in their formal training course, called BUD/S (Basic Underwater Demolition/SEALs). About 20 percent of SEAL candidates quit during Indoc. Those who pass Indoc move on to the first phase of BUD/S.

BUD/S: PHASE ONE

The first phase of BUD/S consists of physical train-ing similar to Indoc. The first phase lasts two months and is made up extreme physical fitness challenges. Recruits swim for miles, go for long runs over sand, and spend hours practicing on an obstacle course.

Recruits are up at 4:30 AM and run everywhere—to meals, to the next training exercise, and to classes. They may run 6 miles (9.7 kilometers) a day, not including their long training runs.

Trainees are constantly sore and tired, and it is not uncommon for a SEAL to break bones or suffer other serious injuries. If a SEAL trainee is injured during

Recruits are subjected to the freezing waters of the Pacific Ocean during Hell Week. Some SEALs get hypothermia, which can cause physical and mental breakdown.

training, he can start over again in a new training class when the injury heals.

Instructors try to make the training as difficult as possible. They make bad conditions even worse. For example, they might spray trainees with cold water during a freezing night training exercise. Instructors need to be sure the trainees are dedicated to becoming SEALs and that they have what it takes to join. BUD/S trainees often hear instructors say, "The only easy day was yesterday." They also hear "It pays to finish first" because men who are the first to finish an exercise, such as a long swim, might get a short break while the rest of the class completes the training task.

Between 20 and 40 percent of men who start the first phase of BUD/S drop out in the first few weeks. Of those who are left, many will quit during Hell Week, which occurs in the fourth week of the first phase. Hell Week is an endurance test for SEAL trainees. If they make it through the week, it proves they are worthy of being trained to become SEALs. During Hell Week, SEAL recruits get very little sleep, usually only an hour or two a night. They must stand in the cold ocean, then run to the beach in their heavy, wet boots and clothes to do push-ups or crawl over wet sand. Then it's back into the freezing water again for a long swim.

Trainees run in small groups over wet sand while carrying a log on their shoulders. Another task is to try to safely land a small boat on a rocky shore while waves pound the boats onto the rocks.

During Hell Week, trainees eat thousands and thousands of calories at four meals a day. But their long hours of extreme exercise and few hours of sleep take a toll. Many men hallucinate and about half quit during the week.

For the men who do make it through Hell Week, the rest of the first phase seems a little easier in comparison. While continuing their physical training, they also learn how to handle boats and scuba dive. They also learn to read maps and create charts.

BUD/S: PHASE TWO

The second phase of BUD/S focuses on diving. For eight weeks recruits learn combat swimming and how to land on shore or get onto ships undetected. They learn how to navigate underwater and how to keep track of how far they have swum. Trainees also get instruction on how to take care of their diving equipment. They also receive some basic medical training. Throughout the second phase, trainees continue with their intense physical training.

Physical training continues through the third phase as well. This last phase of BUD/S is made up of nine weeks of land-warfare training. During the third phase, trainees learn to use a variety of weapons. They also receive instruction on how to blow things up underwater and on land. They learn to work together in small teams and how to plan a mission. They train in how to exit a helicopter using only their gloved hands and boots to rappel down a rope.

SWIMMER DELIVERY VEHICLES

Some SEALs join a swimmer delivery vehicle (SDV) team. SDVs are mini-submarines that can fit two to five people. SEALs use SDVs to secretly reach a shore underwater. The small SDVs are launched from submarines. When operating, the SDVs are filled with freezing deep-ocean water and packed with equipment. Once near their target, the SEALs leave the SDV and swim, underwater, to shore, hauling their equipment. From there, SEALs carry out their mission on land.

SDV operators must be experienced divers and expert swimmers. They must also be mentally and physically tough to withstand long periods of time underwater in cramped and cold spaces.

This swimmer delivery vehicle (SDV) is being prepared for launch from a submarine during a training exercise. SDVs launch from a dry dock shelter (DDS) attached to the back of a submarine.

BUD/S: PHASE THREE

During the last few weeks of the third phase, trainees go to San Clemente Island, off the coast of California. There they put all their skills together in a variety of training exercises. Only about 20 percent of the men who start BUD/S make it to the end of the third phase. Although those men have passed one of the most difficult tests anyone can endure, their training is not done.

After BUD/S, SEAL trainees spend three weeks learning to parachute. At Tactical Air Operations in San Diego, recruits learn various ways to parachute from planes and from helicopters. They practice landing in the water, as well as on land. In many cases during missions, the SEALs will need to parachute with a great deal of gear. Many of their practice jumps include heavy loads of weapons, inflatable boats, and other equipment.

SQT AND BEYOND

Their long months of training continue when SEAL recruits attend SQT, or SEAL Qualification Training. SQT lasts eighteen weeks and is made up of additional specialized training. SEALs learn close quarters defense (CQD) and combat first aid. They learn how to carry out underwater attacks on ships and harbors. The recruits get more training in shooting and small boat operations. They do land-warfare training in the desert and cold-weather training on Kodiak Island, Alaska. If trainees successfully complete SQT, they finally become a SEAL. They receive a gold trident pin, the official Navy SEAL emblem.

On completion of SQT, SEALs are assigned to a SEAL team. SEAL teams are based in three locations: Virginia Beach, Virginia; Coronado, California; and Pearl Harbor, Hawaii. Each team is usually made up of several platoons. Including other personnel that support the team, there are about three hundred people in a SEAL team.

Even after SEALs are assigned to a team, their training continues. Some SEALs go to Special Dive

Cold-weather training on Kodiak Island, Alaska, prepares SEALs for challenges they might face in extreme weather conditions and for problems they could experience with using equipment in low temperatures.

After SERE, SEALs may take the Special Operations Target Interdiction Course (SOTIC), which involves sniper training.

Technician School (SDTS). There they learn to deal with injuries that can occur when diving. Other SEALs attend SERE (Survival, Evasion, Resistance, and Escape) training. This ten-day class teaches SEALs how to avoid being captured by an enemy and what to do if they are captured. They also learn survival techniques, such as how to find water that is safe to drink and how to build fires and shelters. They also learn which plants, animals, and insects are safe to eat and which ones are poisonous.

At the end of SERE, they are sent into the desert with no food or water and are ordered to avoid being captured by instructors who are pretending to be the enemy. If they are captured, the instructors pretend to be prison guards and try to break the SEALs down to obtain information from them. For example, they might try to get a SEAL to give up the location of other team members.

AFTER TRAINING, MORE TRAINING

When SEALs are not on a mission, they are constantly training. Training exercises expand their skills and keep the skills they have already learned fresh. Some classes are attended by individual SEALs or groups of two to three men from a SEAL team. These classes sometimes include special operations forces from other branches of the military.

In these classes, SEALs might take sniper training, which is called Special Operations Target Interdiction Course, or SOTIC. Other classes are for learning advanced driving techniques or foreign language classes. SEALs might also learn how to operate unmanned drones. They can take classes in surveillance and advanced climbing or diving techniques. SEALs can learn how to enter buildings by getting past security systems secretly or using explosives to gain entry.

Other training involves SEALs working together as a unit, brushing up on hand-to-hand combat skills or small-group tactics. They rehearse operations in various environments, such as jungles, deserts, mountains, and urban settings. They also do water training, such as combat swimming, night diving, and submarine operations.

SEALs also take part in joint training exercises with other branches of the military or with other global forces, such as troops from NATO, an international military alliance. These exercises help military forces share knowledge and techniques. They also build cooperation so that everyone will be prepared for future missions.

2

HOSTAGE RESCUES

SEALS PERFORM MANY missions that no one will ever know about. These top-secret missions are never in the news. They're not thanked for their work, and they don't expect to be. They consider a successful mission enough of a reward. There is one kind of mission for which they can receive a very personal and sincere "thank you," however: a hostage rescue mission.

THE RESCUE OF CAPTAIN RICHARD PHILLIPS

In April 2009, pirates off the coast of Somalia hijacked the *Maersk Alabama*, taking several crew members hostage. Pirates had been attacking boats off the coast of Africa for several years, but usually the boats had been small, and the pirates were not always successful in

This photo of the *Maersk Alabama* was taken from a U.S. Navy P-3C Orion aircraft. The P-3C is used for surveillance of ocean-going ships, but it can also detect submarines.

capturing hostages. The *Maersk Alabama* was the first American vessel attacked. The huge container ship, carrying valuable cargo, was headed to several ports in Africa to deliver relief supplies.

To gain entry to the boat, the pirates threw hooks over the railings and climbed ropes to the deck. There they took Captain Richard Phillips, a navigator, and an officer captive. The other seventeen crew members managed to get away and hide. The crew was then able to sink the pirates' boat and, working from below the decks, took back control of the ship's engines. The crew was also able to capture one of the pirates.

The *Maersk* crew tried to trade the pirate they had captured for Captain Phillips. Just as they were about to make the swap, however, the pirates jumped into a lifeboat, taking Captain Phillips with them.

THE RESCUE

To rescue Captain Phillips, the U.S. Navy called in SEAL Team Six. The USS *Bainbridge* and the USS *Boxer* were already in the area, so they quickly

SEAL TEAM SIX TO THE RESCUE

All SEALs are extraordinary, but SEAL Team Six is made up of the best of the best. Also known as DEVGRU, or Naval Special Warfare Development Group, this team is made up of the most highly trained SEALs with the very latest high-tech equipment—in fact, much of the equipment they use is top secret. Members are called in to perform the most challenging missions. The only way to join is to be selected.

In hostage missions, there are several sniper rifles for SEALs to choose from, depending on the job. It is up to the SEAL to pick the right rifle for the task. The SEALs often use Heckler & Koch PSG-2 rifles. They have interchangeable magazines that can hold five, ten, or thirty rounds of ammunition. These rifles can also be set to automatic. They are extremely accurate, which is why they are often the SEALs' top choice.

moved into position near the *Maersk*. The lifeboat holding the pirates and Captain Phillips was small and the water was rough, so the pirates agreed when negotiators on the *Bainbridge* offered to throw them a towline to help keep the boat steady. The towline not only steadied the boat; it also kept it close while the SEALs set up for the rescue.

First, SEAL Team Six had to get to the scene, which was in the middle of the Indian Ocean. To reach the area, the SEALs parachuted from a transport plane into the water, along with inflatable boats.

Two Seawolf submarines coordinated efforts with the USS *Bainbridge* and high-speed SEAL assault vehicles to allow the hostage-takers on the *Maersk* no options.

The SEALs then got on board the *Bainbridge* without being detected by the pirates.

Once on the *Bainbridge* they set up a mobile tactical operations center to communicate with officials in Washington, D.C. Also in the area were two Seawolf submarines and two high-speed SEAL assault vessels. These were moved into position behind the *Boxer*, so the pirates could not see them.

The assault vessels were equipped with grenade launchers and other weapons. Also on the scene were hostage negotiators from the Federal Bureau of Investigation (FBI). They had been flown to the *Bainbridge* to help talk the pirates into releasing Captain Phillips. The pirates wanted $2 million in exchange for returning their hostage.

On the *Bainbridge*, SEAL Team Six began planning how to get Captain Phillips back safely. They had President Barack Obama's approval to shoot the pirates. But they could only do so if Captain Phillips's life seemed to be in danger.

A team of SEAL snipers would constantly monitor the situation in the lifeboat for signs of trouble. Working in four-hour shifts, the SEAL snipers kept their rifles trained on the pirates at all times. When they were not on shift, they slept or kept track of the situation in the tactical operations center. Snipers must be extremely patient, and they must also be constantly on alert.

Snipers usually work in a pair with a spotter. The spotter monitors the target and communicates with other members of the team who are either on- or off-site. The spotter uses a scope to observe the target. Because the job of the sniper requires so much focus, it can get mentally and physically tiring. Usually, during a four-hour shift the sniper and spotter will switch jobs so both can remain alert.

The SEAL snipers on the *Bainbridge* had signaling devices on their rifles. These devices displayed green lights when the sniper had the target in sight. The team commander kept track of the lights on all of the snipers' rifles to make sure they were all ready to go at any given time. They were just waiting for the perfect time to make their shot.

Meanwhile, in the lifeboat with the pirates, Captain Phillips was very hot, tired, and dirty. The pirates had beaten him often, especially after he tried to escape. In their negotiations with officials on the *Bainbridge*, the pirates were threatening to kill the captain. Tensions in the little boat were mounting, and the pirates were fighting among themselves. Then, on the fifth day, one of the pirates fired a shot.

On the *Bainbridge*, hearing the shot, the SEAL snipers sprung into action. Making sure the green lights on the snipers' rifles were on, the team leader gave the command. Each of the snipers fired a shot. With three shots, all three pirates on board the lifeboat were dead. One of the SEALs then slid down the towrope from the *Bainbridge* to the lifeboat to check on Captain Phillips. Happily, Captain Phillips was in good shape and extremely relieved to see the SEAL. Four more SEALs jumped into the high-speed boats

Captain Richard Phillips speaks at a press conference with his son, Dan, by his side after being rescued by Navy SEALs from pirates in 2009.

and sped to the lifeboat to pick up Captain Phillips and their fellow SEAL.

Safely on the *Bainbridge*, Captain Phillips received a checkup and some food. He took a shower and was able to call his family. Captain Phillips also got to meet his SEAL rescuers and personally thank them. In a book about his experience, Captain Phillips said, "I'd always respected the military, but now I really felt how selfless and duty-driven these guys were. They didn't want fame or money or recognition. They just wanted me safe and back with my family." Captain Phillips said he would be grateful for what the SEALs had done for him until the day he died.

The SEALs, too, were happy about the way the mission turned out. One of them told Captain Phillips, "Our missions rarely turn out this way. We train for it to go down exactly as it did yesterday."

THE RESCUE OF JESSICA BUCHANAN AND POUL HAGEN THISTED

On October 25, 2011, two truckloads of pirates captured Jessica Buchanan and Poul Hagen Thisted in Galkayo, Somalia. Buchanan and Thisted worked for a group called the Danish Refugee Council. They were helping educate Somali children about the dangers of weapons. They were also working to remove land mines from the area.

Buchanan, thirty-two, was from Ohio and had been working in Africa for about five years. Thisted, sixty, was from Denmark. They both had just finished a training course and were on their way to the airport in Somalia when they were captured. The pirates took them back to their compound. They demanded a ransom but kept changing their terms for the release of the two hostages.

For months, U.S. government officials worked to free Buchanan and Thisted, with no luck. In the first month that Thisted and Buchanan were held hostage, the U.S. government was not sure where they were. As they gathered information, officials learned more about who the pirates were and where the two captives were being held: a camp near Gadaado, Somalia.

The families of Jessica Buchanan and Poul Hagen Thisted had to keep quiet about their capture or the pirates might have demanded more money as ransom.

As the months dragged on, information the government gathered suggested that Buchanan was sick. The pirates had refused to accept an offer of $1.5 million in ransom. By January, the U.S. government decided to bring in the SEALs. Preparations for the rescue began and on January 23, 2012, President Obama approved the final plan. Once again, SEAL Team Six was called into action.

THE RESCUE

Although the rescue of Captain Phillips took place at sea, in some ways the two hostage situations were similar—armed men were holding the hostages in difficult-to-reach areas. The SEALs would have to act quickly and decisively. Another similarity was that the SEALs would parachute out of an Air Force C-130 transport plane to reach a remote location.

To avoid detection, the SEALs had to jump from a high altitude. High-altitude jumps are difficult and dangerous, but the SEALs are highly trained in this kind of jump. SEALs often jump out of a plane from as high as 30,000 feet (9,144 meters). At this altitude there is not enough oxygen in the air for the SEALs to breathe. They must breathe oxygen through masks while on the plane. They also get oxygen from small containers while jumping.

Another difficulty of high-altitude jumping is the extreme cold. It can be as low as -45° Fahrenheit (-42.7° Celsius), so they wear specialized suits. SEALs practice these types of jumps not only because they are difficult but also because they require precision.

When they jump from the plane, they can reach speeds of well over 200 miles per hour (322 km per hour). Even with these high speeds, the SEALs must land close to each other when they reach the ground so that they do not become separated.

At about 2:00 AM on January 24, 2012, the team silently parachuted out of the C-130. Once they were all on the ground, they had to hike about 3 miles (5 km) through a desertlike area to reach the pirate camp. Taking up positions around the camp, the SEALs used night-vision scopes to see how many people

These SEALs jump from a C-130 Hercules aircraft during a training exercise. The C-130 can carry heavy loads of supplies and even equipment such as helicopters and vehicles.

were in the camp and where they were located. They confirmed the positions of the nine pirates and two hostages. The SEALs also noted that there were explosives in the camp.

The SEALs communicated their findings with off-site team members. An air force plane flying overhead captured video of what was happening on the ground. A team of commanders at the White House watched the video and oversaw the operation.

When the SEALs were confident they had accounted for all the pirates and knew the location of the hostages, they opened fire. The pirates shot back, but within minutes, the nine pirates were dead. The two hostages were unharmed and were now safe. Army Black Hawk helicopters picked up Buchanan and Thisted and their SEAL rescuers. The freed hostages were first taken to an American military base called Camp Lemonnier in Djibouti, Africa. Thisted and Buchanan then went to Naval Air Station Sigonella in Sicily. There, they were reunited with their families.

Buchanan and Thisted's families were thankful for another SEAL job well done. Buchanan said in a statement that she was impressed "by the bravery and heroism of the soldiers who risked their lives to carry it out."

OPERATION RED WINGS: A MISSION GOES WRONG IN AFGHANISTAN

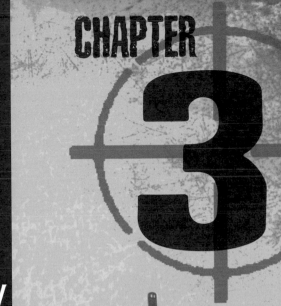

NOT EVERY SEAL MISSION is completely successful. SEAL missions are extremely dangerous, and sometimes even the best-planned operation goes wrong.

In 2005, U.S. military leaders in Afghanistan were on the hunt for Mullah Ahmad Shah. He was an Al Qaeda operative working for Osama bin Laden in the Kunar province of Afghanistan. Shah had killed U.S. troops, and U.S. leaders were hoping to capture him before he killed any more.

The plan was for a team of four SEALs to scout Shah's location and find out how many troops he had with him and what the area was like. Shah was thought to be hiding in a valley, surrounded by mountains and very rugged terrain. Shah and his troops were at an advantage because they knew that area of

Lieutenant Michael Murphy joined the SEALs in July 2002 and had participated in missions in Qatar and Djibouti before leading Operation Red Wings in Afghanistan.

Afghanistan well. The first day of the mission would involve scouting the location. Once the four-man team had located Shah and done their scouting, a larger SEAL team would join them and capture or kill Shah and his forces.

MISSION PREPARATIONS

On June 26, 2005, the four-man SEAL team prepared for their mission, nicknamed Operation Red Wings, after the National Hockey League (NHL) Detroit Red Wings. (At the time, mission planners were using NHL teams as code names for their missions.)

Lieutenant Michael P. Murphy led the team. With him were Petty Officer Second Class Matthew Axelson, Petty Officer Second Class Danny Dietz, and Leading Petty Officer Marcus Luttrell. The Red Wings SEALs gathered their weapons, camouflage clothing, food, and other equipment. Their weapons included four SIG-Sauer 9 mm pistols, two M4 rifles, two Mark 12 .556-caliber rifles, mines, grenades, and plenty of

THERE'S AN APP FOR THAT: MISSION PLANNING SOFTWARE

SEALs use the latest and greatest weapons, communication equipment, and other technology. They even have specially modified software called SOMPE (Special Operations Mission Planning Environment) to help them with their missions. SOMPE allows SEAL teams to communicate securely with each other and with commanders. The software allows them to have private Web chats. It also contains databases full of information they might need to help them plan and carry out their missions.

ammunition. The four SEALs packed nuts, raisins, beef jerky, energy bars, and water. Computers, cameras, communication equipment, medical supplies, and extra batteries for their equipment rounded out their supplies.

PUTTING THE PLAN INTO ACTION

On mission day, Murphy and his team were flown by Chinook MH-47E helicopter to an area in the mountains near where they suspected Shah was hiding. Because they didn't want anyone to see them, the team flew after darkness fell. The Chinook helicopter that took them to the mission can fly up to 154 knots at a maximum altitude of 11,000 feet (3,352 meters). It was equipped with radar, GPS, a satellite communication system, and an infrared device that could "see" warm objects in the dark.

During the flight, the four-man SEAL team went over their mission plan carefully, checked their weapons, and made sure their communication equipment worked. When the helicopter arrived at the designated spot, the pilot found there was no good place to land. Instead, the team would have to do a fast-rope insertion. To accomplish this, the pilot had the helicopter hover over the landing site by pulling up on the nose of the helicopter and lowering the power at the

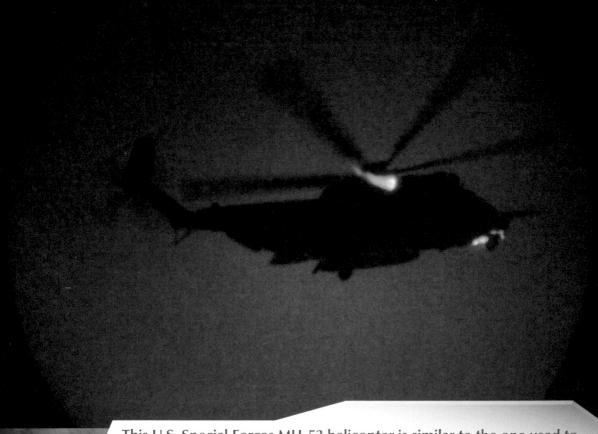

This U.S. Special Forces MH-53 helicopter is similar to the one used to deliver the SEALs to the mission site in Operation Red Wings.

same time. Helicopter support personnel put the platform down at the rear door and clipped a rope to the fast-rope insertion/extraction system, called a FRIES.

The four SEALs put on Kevlar cobra gloves so that the rope wouldn't burn their hands while they were lowering themselves to the ground. They also wore helmets, night-vision goggles, knee and elbow pads, and backpacks loaded with supplies. Each of their backpacks weighed about 85 pounds (38 kilograms).

The four SEALs quickly lowered themselves to the ground by the rope. Once on the ground, nobody moved or talked for the first fifteen minutes. They had to let their vision adjust. They also listened carefully for anyone in the area. They didn't want people on the ground to know that anyone had come out of the helicopter. It was a cold night, and it was raining hard. These were not ideal conditions, but because the moon was not out, at least the chances were good that no one would spot them. The SEAL team took a look around and could see fires burning in the village in the valley below.

After they got their bearings, Murphy, Axelson, Dietz, and Luttrell began climbing the mountain to find a good hiding spot for the day ahead. The climb was very difficult, even for the SEALs, who were experienced climbers. The rain made it even more difficult.

The SEALs climbed for about seven hours, until they found what they thought would be a good hiding spot for the day. Their spot allowed them to see the village in the valley below. However, some fog rolled in and soon they couldn't see the village at all. They were forced to look for a new hiding spot, which they found after about an hour. The new spot was not perfect because there were not many trees or rocks to hide behind. Also, there was only one way out of the hiding spot—down the mountain. The sun was coming up soon, though, so they settled there.

Their hiding spot proved to be worse than they thought when they were discovered by three Afghan goatherds, one of whom was a teenaged boy. The SEALs had a long discussion about what to do with the three Afghans. If they let them go, the men might tell Shah about their location. However, the SEALs didn't want to kill two innocent men and a teenager. The SEALs decided to let them go. But letting them go meant they would have to move, even though it was the middle of the day. They returned to the hiding spot they had left because of the fog, which by then had burned off. The SEALs settled in to try to locate Shah in the village below and to wait for darkness.

THINGS GO WRONG

About an hour and a half after settling into their new hiding spot, the team was suddenly surrounded on three sides by Shah's men. There were more than one hundred fighters, armed with AK-47 machine guns. Some had rocket-propelled grenades (RPGs). An intense firefight broke out, but the SEALs were completely outnumbered and knew they wouldn't be able to hold off the Afghan fighters for long. The only way out was to try to make their way down the rocky slope, shooting at the Afghans at the same time.

The mountain was steep, and there were few hiding spots. The Afghan fighters fired on them nonstop, and the SEALs returned fire continuously. Soon all four men were wounded, most of them having been shot multiple times. The four SEALs continued to battle the Afghan forces while trying to make their way down the mountain. Murphy attempted to contact their commanders to let them know their situation, but he wasn't able to establish a communication link.

When things go wrong during missions in enemy territory, the SEALs are exposed to extreme dangers, such as these Taliban forces.

Murphy knew by then that the only way to save his team was to contact the base to be rescued. The only way to do that was to get out in the open so that he could get a signal on his satellite phone. So he left his hiding spot, knowing that he would be shot and probably killed. Murphy was able to contact his commanders but was shot multiple times and killed.

Soon, only Luttrell was left alive, although he was badly injured. He had been blasted by an RPG into a hole, upside down. This was extremely lucky for Luttrell because he was hidden from the Afghan fighters.

Operation Red Wings included team members *(from left to right)* Matthew Axelson, Daniel Healy, James Suh, Marcus Luttrell, Eric Patton, and Michael Murphy.

However, he had serious injuries and no longer had his medical supplies or water with him.

A BAD SITUATION GETS WORSE

Back at the base, the commanders who received the communication from Murphy scrambled to put together a rescue team. Soon, two helicopters filled with SEALs and other special operations forces were on the way to try to rescue the four SEALs. Once at the landing site, the situation went from bad to worse. Afghan fighters on the ground fired an RPG at the helicopters, shooting one down. All eight SEALs and eight Army Rangers on board were killed. The other helicopter was forced to head back to base, without rescuing any of the four Operation Red Wings SEALs.

Meanwhile, on the ground, Luttrell remained hidden in the hole for about a day. The following night, he left his hiding spot because he desperately needed to find water. It took him more than a day to find water, and while he was looking he was shot at again. Eventually, he not only found water but was spotted by some Afghan villagers who decided to help him. They kept him hidden from Shah's fighters and gave him food. They also found a doctor to help him. Finally, six days after arriving on the mountain, a team of U.S. Army Rangers and Green Berets rescued Luttrell. The rescue team was also able to locate the bodies of Murphy, Axelson, and Dietz. Shah escaped but was eventually killed by Pakistani police in 2008.

MEDAL OF HONOR

The Medal of Honor is the highest military award for bravery and going "above and beyond the call of duty." On October 22, 2007, Michael P. Murphy was given the honor and his family accepted it on his behalf.

Since the Vietnam War, only eight people have been awarded this honor, all of whom died in the line of duty. Murphy was the fourth SEAL to receive this award. He was the first Medal of Honor winner for combat operations in Afghanistan. To further honor him, in 2008 the U.S. Navy named an Arleigh Burke–class guided-missile destroyer the USS *Michael Murphy*.

President George W. Bush hands the Medal of Honor to Michael Murphy's mother, Maureen Murphy, at a White House ceremony.

OPERATION NEPTUNE SPEAR: KILLING OSAMA BIN LADEN

THE HUNT FOR OSAMA bin Laden lasted for almost ten years. Governments from several countries put in serious efforts to find him. Once they did, it was up to SEAL Team Six to capture him.

Osama bin Laden, the founder of the terrorist group Al Qaeda, is considered the mastermind of the attacks on the United States on September 11, 2001. When he was identified as the person who had planned and financed the attacks, the U.S. government and other governments around the world began hunting for him. They all worked to bring him to justice. However, no one could locate him. He was reported to be in many locations, but searches for him always came up empty.

Until his death on May 2, 2011, by SEAL Team Six, Osama bin Laden was the most wanted and dangerous terrorist in the world.

In September 2008, the U.S. government heard that bin Laden might be in a small town called Angoor Ada in Pakistan. A SEAL operation was launched to capture him, but he was not there. Many believed he was already dead.

FOUND?

In January 2011, the Central Intelligence Agency (CIA) thought they might have learned where bin Laden was hiding. They had intelligence that he was living in a walled compound in Abbottabad, Pakistan. Satellites had taken pictures of a man of bin Laden's height (he was between 6 feet 4 inches and 6 feet 6 inches [1.93 m and 1.98 m] tall) living there. They had also picked up voice communications from the compound that were a 60–70 percent match for bin Laden's voice. Although they were not positive it was bin Laden, they began to put together a plan to raid the compound.

The SEAL Team Six commanding officer was called to CIA headquarters in Washington, D.C., to meet with military and CIA officials. They began drawing up a plan. The operation would need to include helicopters because the compound was in Pakistan. Since Pakistan is a country not friendly to the United States, they would not allow military planes to land there or troops to assemble on the ground. Helicopters would have to fly the SEALs in from a neighboring country.

PLANNING THE OPERATION

It took several months to plan the operation. During that time, survcillance of the compound continued. The CIA tried to gather more information about who lived there. They also wanted to know what their habits were, such as when they usually went to bed or what days they left the compound to shop for food.

While surveillance continued, SEAL Team Six was hard at work planning and practicing the mission. Based on the information they continued to receive from the CIA, they planned every aspect of the operation. How would they get there? How many SEALs would go? Would any non-SEALs go along? How would they enter the compound? How would they search for bin Laden once on the ground? What weapons would they need? Surveillance had indicated that there were about thirty people living in the compound. Some of them were women and children. SEALs knew that it would be very confusing once they entered the compound. With that many other people inside, their operation had to be perfectly planned so that no one would be harmed.

The mission had to be practiced over and over again. This practice was like a rehearsal before the mission. SEALs sometimes practice at Tall Pines, a top-secret army and SEAL training site hidden in a forest somewhere on the East Coast of the United States. At Tall Pines, SEAL teams build full-scale models of their mission sites. There they can act out their missions in a realistic setting so that they will be fully prepared for the real thing. SEAL Team Six

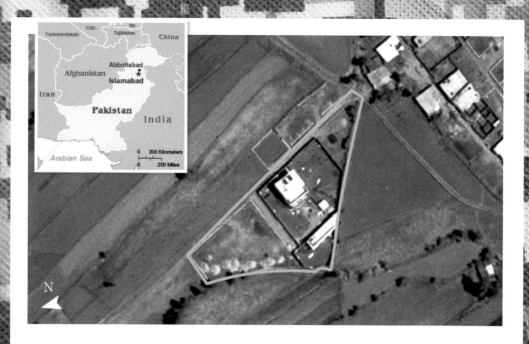

The compound in Abbottabad, Pakistan, where Osama bin Laden was living during his final days was heavily fortified.

practiced for the bin Laden mission at Tall Pines, in a replica of the Pakistan compound.

GEARING UP FOR THE MISSION

In late April, SEAL Team Six and support personnel and officials gathered at Jalalabad Air Base in Afghanistan. Also at Jalalabad were four MH-47 Chinook helicopters, two Stealth Hawk helicopters, and two Ghost Hawk helicopters. In the air overhead were four satellites. One satellite monitored the weather and one was devoted to communications.

THE HAWKS

SEAL teams use two types of extremely high-tech helicopters: Stealth Hawks and Ghost Hawks. Ghost Hawks are top secret and used only by SEAL Team Six and SEAL Team Delta. They are flown only at night and are kept under lock and key. They are very quiet in the air and can't be seen on radar. They don't put out much heat, so they cannot be seen easily by thermal sensors.

Stealth Hawks are a slightly older model than Ghost Hawks and don't have as many high-tech features. Because military officials didn't want to risk the Ghost Hawks getting shot down in enemy territory, Stealth Hawks were used for the Neptune Spear mission.

One captured regular, infrared, or ultraviolet images. The fourth satellite could do any of the three tasks. A RQ-170 Sentinel drone was also in the air. This drone can't be seen on radar and flies only at night. It took incredibly clear videos of the compound. The pictures were so clear that people monitoring the video on the ground could tell whether the sliding glass door where SEALs planned to enter the main building of the compound was open or closed.

At Jalalabad, SEALs participating in the mission to get bin Laden made their preparations. They gathered their supplies, including weapons and explosives. The explosives could be used to blast holes in the compound walls. Once in the compound, the SEALs would use more explosives to gain entry into the buildings. The SEALs fully expected to be shot at by bin Laden and his security forces, so they all would wear extensive body armor.

In addition to the SEALs, a CIA interpreter would accompany them. The interpreter could help them speak to people in the compound. Also on the mission would be Karo, a highly trained dog. Karo, a Belgian Malinois, would wear specially made body armor and goggles. These would protect him from bullets and explosives. Karo was trained to detect explosives, so he could sniff out potential dangers once the SEALs were on the ground.

The SEALs went over their plan again and again. Once they were at the compound, one Stealth Hawk helicopter would land on the roof of the main building. The other Stealth Hawk would provide cover

NOT ALL SEALS ARE HUMAN

Among the many tools available to help SEALs do their jobs are highly trained dogs. The main job of SEAL dogs is to detect improvised explosive devices (IEDs). The dogs can also track down hidden enemy forces or catch suspects trying to get away. Like their human counterparts, SEAL dogs are highly trained and only the very best dogs complete their training and go on to join a SEAL team. SEALs who work with dogs get specialized training, including basic veterinary care. The dog breeds most often used on SEAL teams are German shepherds, Belgian Malinois, and Dutch shepherds.

fire for anyone shooting at the first Hawk. When the SEALs from the first Hawk were inside the main building, the second Hawk would land on the roof of the guesthouse.

OPERATION NEPTUNE SPEAR

At 10:00 PM on May 1, 2011, the two Stealth Hawk helicopters took off from Jalalabad Air Base. The two Hawks flew low to the ground at 130 miles per hour (209 km per hour). While they were in the air, an EA-6B Prowler jammed Pakistani radar so that the Stealth Hawks wouldn't be detected. The two helicopters had to stop to refuel at the Afghanistan-Pakistan border, so two MH-47 helicopters set up there with refueling equipment.

Hunting down Osama bin Laden

The raid that killed al-Qaida leader Osama bin Laden took shape after detainees identified a bin Laden courier.

First information

• After 9/11, CIA chases leads about bin Laden's inner circle

• Detainees repeatedly mention one courier's pseudonym, identifying him as one of the few trusted by bin Laden; true name, location unknown

• Courier's true identity learned in 2007

• Two years later, locations where courier and his brother operate in Pakistan are learned

Narrowing in

• **August 2010** Courier's residence found: high-security compound in Abbottabad, Pakistan

September 2010 U.S. thinks bin Laden may be hiding in compound

February 2011 U.S. thinks intelligence is strong enough to begin developing plan for going after bin Laden

March 2011 First of five National Security Council meetings on capturing or killing bin Laden; other meetings: March 29, April 12, April 19, April 28

The operation

• **April 29, 2011, 8:20 a.m. EDT** Obama authorizes operation

• **May 1, 1 p.m.** Top advisers gather at White House

• **Around 3 p.m. (midnight in Pakistan)** Helicopters heard over Abbottabad

• Two dozen Navy SEALs drop into high-walled compound; inside for 40 minutes

• Bin Laden killed in last five or 10 minutes of siege; shot twice in the head on third floor of main building

Inside the compound in Abbottabad

• Built in 2005; about 3,000 sq. ft. (279 sq. m) of space; but no telephone or Internet service to avoid detection

• Two men lived on first floor

• Exterior walls topped with barbed wire

Jalalabad U.S. helicopters fly on raid mission

Abbottabad Al-Qaida leader Osama bin Laden killed by U.S. forces

CHINA

AFGHAN.

Kabul ★ ○ ○ ○ ●

Peshawar ★ Islamabad

Ghazi Air Base Additional forces fly from here

INDIA

200 km

200 miles

PAKISTAN

PAKISTAN

Opaque windows (north side)

Wall 11 ft. (3.4 m) high

Wall 10 ft. (3 m) high

Gate

Privacy wall 7 ft. (2.1 m) high

2005 aerial image of the compound

Where trash was burned

Gate

NORTH

Wall 18 ft. (5.5 m) high

Bin Laden and family lived on second and third floor; cleared last

Forces fought through first floor where two adult males lived

Wall 12 ft. (3.7 m) high

Outcome and aftermath All times EDT

• One U.S. helicopter lost because of mechanical failure; destroyed for security purposes

• Along with bin Laden, three adult males killed: bin Laden's son and two al-Qaida facilitators

• Woman identified as bin Laden's wife used as human shield, killed; two others injured

• **3:32 p.m.** Obama returns for update

• **3:50 p.m.** Obama told bin Laden appears to be one of those killed during raid

• **11:35 p.m.** After confirmation, Obama announces in televised address that U.S. forces killed bin Laden and are in custody of his body

• Bin Laden's body put aboard the USS Carl Vinson, then placed in the North Arabian Sea

Sources: U.S. Government, The White House, AP, Reuters, ESRI, National Journal.com   Graphic: Robert Dorrell, Judy Treible, Melina Yingling   © 2011 MCT

Operation Neptune Spear was a major operation that required flawless planning, not only from the Navy SEALs but also from President Obama himself.

Three hours after leaving Jalalabad, the first Stealth Hawk was hovering over the roof of the main house of the compound. Although they had planned to land the helicopter, when they arrived on scene they found there was not enough space for the helicopter to land. There was no time to change the plan and land somewhere else in the compound.

The SEALs had to jump from the Stealth Hawk onto the roof instead. In just seconds, the SEALs had jumped to the roof, then down to the terrace. Seconds after that they went into the house through the open sliding glass door. Inside, the SEALs spread out through the house, remembering their hours of training at the replica of the house at Tall Pines.

Soon, one of the SEALs spotted Osama bin Laden peeking his head out of a doorway. Bin Laden slammed the door shut but two of the SEALs kicked the door in and entered the room. Within seconds, the SEALs had shot bin Laden and he was dead.

Although their primary mission was accomplished, Operation Neptune Spear was not quite done. The SEALs had to carefully clear the compound, rounding up the rest of the people. They secured the people and left them for local officials, who would decide what to do with them. SEALs also went through the main house gathering computers and documents. These could provide information about bin Laden's future terrorist plans. The SEALs also took bin Laden's body, to confirm it was actually him through DNA testing. (The next day, the SEALs buried him at sea.)

All had gone according to plan during Neptune Spear, but then one of the Hawks crashed. Although no one was hurt, the helicopter had to be destroyed. Because the Stealth Hawk was full of top-secret, high-tech gear, it could not just be left, where it could fall into the wrong hands. The SEALs had to smash all of the equipment inside, and then they blew it up. Some of the SEALs left the compound in the other Stealth Hawk helicopter. Others waited for a backup Chinook helicopter to fly in from Jalalabad to retrieve them.

The tail of the downed Stealth Hawk helicopter was all that remained after SEAL Team Six destroyed the wreckage to protect its top-secret technology.

SEAL Team Six had just accomplished what many around the world had been trying to do for many years. They didn't receive any personal recognition because the identity of SEALs is such a closely guarded secret. They were just satisfied their mission had been a success and that no one had been injured. For them, it was just another day on the job. Being a SEAL is no ordinary job, but SEALs certainly treat it as though it is.

GLOSSARY

ALLY A person or group that shares a common goal.

AMBUSH To attack from a hidden position.

COMPOUND An enclosed area containing a group of buildings.

DATABASE A collection of information organized in various ways.

DRONE An aircraft that does not have a pilot.

HALLUCINATE To imagine hearing or seeing things that aren't really there.

HORMONE A substance that regulates various body functions.

IMPROVISED EXPLOSIVE DEVICE (IED) A homemade bomb not manufactured by or for a military.

INDOCTRINATION A period of general training.

INFRARED Red light that cannot be seen by the human eye.

INTELLIGENCE Information about an enemy.

LAND MINES Explosives that are buried underground.

MAGAZINE A container that holds gun cartridges.

METRONOMIC Perfectly regulated.

NEGOTIATOR A person who tries to bring about an agreement between two parties.

NEUROTRANSMITTER A substance that carries information from one brain neuron to another.

PLATOON A subset of a military group.

RAPPEL To descend from something by sliding down a rope.

RECONNAISSANCE Exploring enemy territory to gather information.

REPLICA An exact, or near-exact, copy of something.

ROCKET-PROPELLED GRENADE (RPG) A large antitank weapon that can be fired by steadying it on a person's shoulder.

SURVEILLANCE To have someone or something under close watch.

TOWROPE A line used to tow something.

ULTRAVIOLET Violet light that cannot be seen by the human eye.

FOR MORE INFORMATION

Navy Recruiting Command
5722 Integrity Drive, Building 784
Millington, TN 38054
(800) USA-NAVY (872-6289)
Web site: http://www.navy.com
The main site for the U.S. Navy has information on joining
  and serving in the navy.

Navy SEAL Foundation
1619 D Street, Building 5326
Virginia Beach, VA 23459
(757) 363-7490
Web site: http://nswfoundation.org
The Navy SEAL Foundation helps SEALs and their families
  cope with the demands of duty.

SEAL + SWCC Scout Team
2000 Trident Way, Building #613
San Diego, CA 92155
(888) USN-SEAL (876-7325)
Web site: http://www.sealswcc.com
The official site of the Navy SEALs offers information on
  recruiting, missions, and training.

U.S. Department of Defense
1400 Defense Pentagon
Washington, DC 20301-1400

Web site: http://www.defense.gov
The U.S. Department of Defense oversees all branches of
the military.

U.S. Special Operations Command (USSOCOM)
7701 Tampa Point Boulevard
MacDill Air Force Base, FL 33621-5323
Web site: http://www.socom.mil
USSOCOM manages all special operations missions for
the U.S. government.

WEB SITES

Due to the changing nature of Internet links, Rosen
Publishing has developed an online list of Web sites
related to the subject of this book. This site is updated
regularly. Please use this link to access the list:

http://www.rosenlinks.com/ISF/SEALS

FOR FURTHER READING

Bahmanyar, Mir, and Chris Osman. *SEALs: The US Navy's Elite Fighting Force*. Long Island City, NY: Osprey Publishing, 2008.

Bessel, Jennifer M. *The Navy SEALs*. Minneapolis, MN: Bellwether Media, 2009.

David, Jack. *Navy SEALs*. Mankato, MN: Capstone Press, 2011.

Farndon, John. *Special Forces*. Thaxted, England: Miles Kelly Publishing, 2010.

Goldish, Meish. *War Dogs*. New York, NY: Bearport Publishing, 2012.

Greitens, Eric. *The Heart and the Fist: The Education of a Humanitarian, the Making of a Navy SEAL*. Boston, MA: Houghton Mifflin Harcourt, 2011.

Hamilton, John. *Special Forces*. Edina, MN: Checkerboard Books, 2007.

Labrecque, Ellen. *Special Forces*. Mankato, MN: Heinemann-Raintree, 2012.

Lunis, Natalie. *The Takedown of Osama bin Laden*. New York, NY: Bearport Publishing, 2012.

Luttrell, Marcus, and Patrick Robinson. *Lone Survivor: The Eyewitness Account of Operation Redwing and the Lost Heroes of SEAL Team 10*. New York, NY: Little, Brown and Company, 2007.

Nelson, Drew. *Navy SEALs*. New York, NY: Gareth Stevens Publishing, 2012.

Rudolph, Jessica. *Today's Navy Heroes*. New York, NY: Bearport Publishing, 2012.

Smith, Stewart. *The Complete Guide to Navy Seal Fitness*. 3rd ed. Long Island City, NY: Hatherleigh Press, 2008.

Wachtel, Roger. *The Medal of Honor*. New York, NY: Scholastic Books, 2009.

Williams, Brian. *Special Forces*. Mankato, MN: Heinemann-Raintree, 2011.

Yomtov, Nel. *Navy SEALs in Action*. New York, NY: Bearport Publishing, 2008.

Zimmerman, Dwight Jon, and John D. Gresham. *Uncommon Valor: The Medal of Honor and the Six Warriors Who Earned It in Iraq and Afghanistan*. New York, NY: St. Martin's Press, 2010.

BIBLIOGRAPHY

Alcindor, Yamiche. "Somalia Hostage's Husband Cites 'Three Months of Hell.'" *USA Today*, January 26, 2012. Retrieved January 31, 2012 (http://www.usatoday.com/news/world/story/2012-01-26/somalia-hostages/52803954/1).

Bahmanyar, Mir, and Chris Osman. *SEALs: The US Navy's Elite Fighting Force*. Long Island City, NY: Osprey Publishing, 2008.

Barnes, Julian E., Nathan Hodge, and Adam Entous. "Navy SEALs Rescue Hostages in Somalia: Night Mission Leaves 9 Captors Dead, After Weeks of White House Planning." *Wall Street Journal*, January 26, 2012. Retrieved January 31, 2012 (http://online.wsj.com/article/SB10001424052970203806504577182422284560592.html).

Couch, Dick. *Down Range: Navy SEALs in the War on Terrorism*. New York, NY: Crown Publishers, 2005.

Greitens, Eric. *The Heart and the Fist: The Education of a Humanitarian, the Making of a Navy SEAL*. Boston, MA: Houghton Mifflin Harcourt, 2011.

Klaidman, Daniel. "Navy SEALs: Obama's Secret Army." *Newsweek*, February 20, 2012. Retrieved March 1, 2012 (http://www.thedailybeast.com/newsweek/2012/02/19/navy-seals-obama-s-secret-army.html).

Luttrell, Marcus, and Patrick Robinson. *Lone Survivor: The Eyewitness Account of Operation Redwing and the Lost Heroes of SEAL Team 10*. New York, NY: Little, Brown and Company, 2007.

Mann, Don, and Ralph Pezzullo. *Inside SEAL Team Six: My Life and Missions with America's Elite Warriors*. New York, NY: Little, Brown and Company, 2011.

McFadden, Robert D., and Scott Shane. "In Rescue of Captain, Navy Kills 3 Pirates." *New York Times*, April 13, 2009. Retrieved January 4, 2012 (http://www.nytimes.com/2009/04/13/world/africa/13pirates.html?pagewanted=all).

Pfarrer, Chuck. *SEAL Target Geronimo: The Inside Story of the Mission to Kill Osama Bin Laden*. New York, NY: St. Martin's Press, 2011.

Phillips, Richard, and Stephan Talty. *A Captain's Duty: Somali Pirates, Navy SEALs, and Dangerous Days at Sea*. New York, NY: Hyperion, 2010.

Scott Tyson, Ann. "How SEALs Carried Out Their Mission." *Washington Post*, April 13, 2009. Retrieved January 4, 2012 (http://www.washingtonpost.com/wp-dyn/content/article/2009/04/12/AR2009041202645.html).

WARCOM Public Affairs. "SDV Missions." *Ethos*, Issue 12, pp. 10–12.

Wasdin, Howard E., and Stephen Templin. *SEAL Team Six: Memoirs of an Elite Navy SEAL Sniper*. Annapolis, MD: Naval Institute Press, 2011.

Williams, Gary. *SEAL of Honor: Operation Red Wings and the Life of Lt. Michael P. Murphy, USN*. New York, NY: St. Martin's Press, 2010.

Zimmerman, Dwight Jon, and John D. Gresham. *Uncommon Valor: The Medal of Honor and the Six Warriors Who Earned It in Iraq and Afghanistan*. New York, NY: St. Martin's Press, 2010.

INDEX

ABOUT THE AUTHOR

Simone Payment has a degree in psychology from Cornell University and a master's degree in elementary education from Wheelock College. She is the author of twenty-seven books for young adults. Her previous book about Navy SEALs, *Inside Special Operations: Navy SEALs*, won a 2004 Quick Picks for Reluctant Young Readers award from the American Library Association and is on the Nonfiction Honor List of Voice of Youth Advocates.

PHOTO CREDITS